Spooky Brews For The Soul

Spooky Brews For The Soul

Dear Midnight Seeker,

Step into the realm of eerie introspection, where the haunting season invites you to embark on a delightful yet chilling inner journey. Within this 31-day gratitude journal, you'll find spooky contemplations designed to enchant you in mystery and profound reflection. Each page unveils a unique narrative, blending eeriness with charm as you explore different aspects of your identity. Accompanying these reflections are uplifting affirmations, offering daily inspiration for self-empowerment. May this enchanting little book positively influence your inner quest, fostering valuable insights, self-love, and self-connection—all while infusing your journey with ghostly fun!

Happy Haunted Journaling!

Contents

"You are not a body. You have a body. This is just a suit of clothes, a costume you're wearing right now to play this part."

—Dolores Cannon

Day 1: Threads of Destiny

As darkness falls, tales of the mystical fox awaken. On one fateful night, the ghostly fox calls for you to follow, its gentle glow guiding you deep into the woods. The air is thick with earthy, wild scents that send shivers down your spine. In a moonlit clearing, a giant, twisted tree reveals a hidden library within its trunk—countless books fill your sight while tiny wisps of glimmering light illuminate your path. As you lose yourself in a moment of enchanting exploration, the spectral fox leads you to a particular section of books. Curiously, you run your fingers over their spines, seeking one that pulsates with energy. With eyes closed, you make your pick, and upon opening them, you read the title "In the Labyrinth of Fate." Turning to a random page, you encounter the following passage:

"Given the possibility that multiple destinies await your alignment, what, in your eyes, paves the way to a remarkable one?"

Take a moment to contemplate this evocative passage, sharing your reflections on the factors that could shape a distinctive and remarkable life path.

I am grateful for:

1. _____

2. _____

3. _____

Every choice I make aligns me with a destiny filled with love, peace, joy, and fulfillment.

Day 2: Cauldron of Dreams

Imagine a cauldron of dreams brewing before you, possibilities swirling in a mixture of every color. What visions would you see within its bubbling surface, resonating deeply with your heart?

I am grateful for:

1. _____

2. _____

3. _____

I am a co-creator of my destiny.

Day 3: Tales of the Patch

Picture yourself in a pumpkin patch surrounded by hundreds of Jack-o-lanterns. From large to tiny squashes, each pumpkin is carved with a distinct expression. Some appear happy, sad, or angry, while others look crazy, mischievous, and even whimsical. They come in various colors and wear special attire, including hats, flowers, twinkling lights, and more.

Contemplate the jack-o-lantern of your choice and share the reasons behind your selection. What kind of face would your pumpkin wear, and what special features would it display? Furthermore, what about this jack-o-lantern resonates deeply with you?

If you're feeling artistic, feel free to sketch, design a collage, or craft your chosen pumpkin.

I am grateful for:

1. _____

2. _____

3. _____

Day 4: Secrets in the Wind

Suppose the wind could carry a message on your behalf. What words would it say, and to whom? How would the wind convey your thoughts? Would it manifest as a whisper, an eerie whistle, or a spine-chilling wail in the night? And if the recipient inquired about the sender, what details would you entrust the wind to reveal?

I am grateful for:

1. _____

2. _____

3. _____

Every word I speak carries the weight of my truth and sincerity.

Day 5: The Chilling Portrait

Within the corridors of a haunted museum, renowned for its paranormal encounters, you find yourself captivated by a looming portrait of a famous historical figure. As you curiously study the details of the painting, the being's eyes somehow meet your gaze.

Startled and frightened by this unexpected encounter, you stumble backward to the ground. Unnerved, you look up to see the painted figure still locking eyes with you. In a probing tone and an accent from many years past, it asks the following questions:

"Do you believe every individual has a specific purpose or role to fulfill within their lifetime? What are the reasons behind your perspective, and if you align with this view, what do you believe your own role entails?"

Take a moment to imagine the historical entity depicted in the portrait. Who would you choose for such a chilling yet riveting encounter, and why? Afterward, contemplate their questions and share your reflections.

I am grateful for:

1. _____

2. _____

3. _____

I find strength in moments of uncertainty, trusting in my ability to adapt and thrive.

Day 6: Webbie's Guidance

As rain taps gently against the windowpane, you are seated at a lovely, quaint table, sipping sweet bubble tea with your spider friend, Webbie. You begin to share a situation that has been haunting your thoughts, while Webbie listens intently, perched on the rim of her teacup.

As you conclude your story, a sudden shift occurs. You are no longer in a cozy setting but trapped within layers of silken web. You panic, push, and struggle to escape the cocoon you find yourself in. Confused and desperate, you call out to Webbie for help. Her calm voice echoes in your mind, explaining that the web responds to resistance, and the more you fight, the tighter it clings.

Webbie shares that as long as you attach to unsettling, self-fabricated concepts, you will remain trapped within an imaginary, troubling existence. She reassures you that the web enveloping you will dissolve once you determine that which you are identifying with. Only then will self-awareness unfold, enabling a truly conscious choice. She adds that fear, panic, and adverse thoughts only strengthen and multiply the layers of the web.

Webbie advises harnessing lovely thoughts and emotions within yourself, letting them sink into your subconscious to transform your reality and free you from your own metaphorical webs.

Pause momentarily to consider Webbie's words and reflect on any false identities you've been unwittingly embracing as truth—even as you resist them. Observe your thoughts, recognizing that you are separate from them. Like passing clouds in the sky, your thoughts are transient; you are the observer, simply watching, liberated from the need to attach and identify with them.

When you are ready, redirect your attention to the genuine aspects of yourself that kindle inspiration and contentment—those elements of clarity and joy that resonate deeply with your true essence. Then, take a moment to capture these reflections in writing.

I am grateful for:

1. _____

2. _____

3. _____

I release the need for control and surrender to the flow of life, embracing feelings of love and joy.

Day 7: Spirited Journeys

Imagine finding yourself face-to-face with the paranormal. What kind of experience would you seek, and what profound insights or knowledge would you hope to gain from it?

Alternatively, if you have encountered such phenomena, please share the insights you received through your experiences. How did these events influence or transform you?

I am grateful for:

1. _____

2. _____

3. _____

I embrace the unknown with excitement and curiosity.

Day 8: Grim Guidance

Embark on an intriguing exploration of your inner world by connecting with a spooky creature. Below, you'll find a curated list of haunting characters to choose from, each serving as a unique creative avenue for self-reflection.

Among the following, which eerie being captures your attention? What does it symbolize to you, and why do you believe it represents you personally? Furthermore, if this being could share its wisdom or guidance with you today, what message do you imagine it conveying? (If none of the following options resonate with you, feel free to choose a different character for self-reflection.)

Ghost   Scarecrow   Vampire   Werewolf   Witch

I am grateful for:

1. _____

2. _____

3. _____

In moments of unease and mystery, I cultivate deeper layers of self-awareness and growth.

Day 9: A Ghostly Reunion

One night, while deep in your slumber, something jolts you awake. Startled, you sit up and look around. As your eyes adjust to your surroundings, you notice an odd, soft radiance on the floor—a small sphere of light. With a racing heart, you pick up the glowing ball and study it closely.

All of a sudden, a strange feeling sweeps over you as if someone is watching. Your focus shifts from the mysterious ball to the space before you, where you perceive a faint, translucent being—a ghostly child.

You can't believe your eyes, and as you look closer, the child's appearance is hauntingly familiar. It's a young version of you from a time of profound significance. In a gentle voice, the child reveals they have 24 hours to visit.

What activities would you plan for your time together? Select an age with deep meaning and create a list of exciting things to do. Once you've completed your list, consider engaging in one of these activities and reconnecting with your inner child.

Furthermore, if inner healing is needed, welcome this opportunity to reflect on a childhood memory that left a lasting impression, whether it brought forth a sense of delight or presented challenges. What would you express to your ghost child about that time? Compose a letter and embrace the act of reading it aloud, allowing your words to resonate, bringing solace and understanding to both you and the spectral memory of your younger self.

I am grateful for:

1. _____

2. _____

3. _____

As I connect with my inner child, I release old wounds and invite a profound sense of healing and self-love.

Day 10: Whimsical Wizardry

Visualize yourself as a caster of eerie and enchanting spells; what incantations would you utter to transform your reality? Let the power of your words resound by creating playful chants that align with your deepest desires. Once you've crafted your mystical spells, recite them aloud using the magic of intention, letting the air carry your wishes out into the universe.

You are welcome to embrace any of the following spells that resonate with you, reveling in their positive influence. Moreover, if you're feeling inspired and whimsically enchanted, craft your own magical experience. Light some candles, brew your favorite drinks, burn soothing scents, and recite affirming spells, forging a moment of empowerment and manifestation.

Zing-Zong, somber skies, through every trial, I joyfully rise!

Woos and woes of my ghostly past: be buried, be banished, let joy amass!

Whispering winds of fear and doubt, I cast you away with love that abounds!

Hooting owls and rustling leaves, grant me luck that never leaves!

Blazing stars, flickering flames, bestow upon me some winning aims!

Magic mirrors and hidden doors, lead me to bliss and peaceful shores!

Moonlight whispers, fates untold, weave me a path of silver and gold!

I am grateful for:

1. _____

2. _____

3. _____

I trust in the power of my intentions, knowing that the universe listens to the enchantment within my words.

Day 11: Contemplating Life's Endgame

Imagine playing chess with the Grim Reaper at a small, elegant table in the middle of a lush green grassland. As the Reaper takes a turn, you ponder the thousands of dead bodies resting beneath the ground. Before you can make your next move, the Reaper distracts you with thought-provoking questions:

"Is the experience of dying a profound lesson? What do you believe is gained or learned from the dying process and death itself?"

"Considering that your body has an expiration date, how might this awareness influence you? Can you find gratitude and beauty in the inevitable end of the physical plane? What insights emerge as you ponder the final moments of this existence?"

Take a moment to consider these profound questions posed by your grim chess opponent, and share your reflections.

I am grateful for:

1. _____

2. _____

3. _____

Knowing that my life is temporary encourages me to live authentically, embracing the gifts of this world.

Day 12: A Dive into Captivating Realms

Do you believe in nonphysical realities? What kinds of intangible phenomena and realms do you imagine exist? Consider the presence of invisible interactions and forces that may shape this world. What are your thoughts on the otherworldly, encompassing the supernatural, extraterrestrials, fantasy, and so on, and its influence in our lives that the naked eye cannot see?

I am grateful for:

1. _____

2. _____

3. _____

I celebrate the wonders that enrich my life, finding excitement in unseen possibilities.

Day 13: Tears of Trials

Trapped within a black-and-white realm, you hear the mournful wails of a banshee echoing through a desolate landscape. Pulled by an invisible force, you are led toward the haunting cries. Beneath the shade of an angel oak tree, you see the banshee resting on a rock, consumed by profound sorrow. Her long, black hair sways gently in the breeze—and as she gazes up at you, her tears glisten with color, reminiscent of the hues in soap bubbles.

In a spectral voice, she presents a series of questions:

"How can I create inner peace when I am often the source of my pain?"

"Must I wait for my deathbed to reshape the perception of my trials? How might impending death alter the perception of my challenges?"

"What encompasses the phenomenon where resistance to challenges magnifies their presence? What is the secret to flipping the script and reclaiming personal power?"

"What perspectives might you embrace to distance yourself from the impact of your trials?"

As the banshee awaits your responses, seated mournfully on the rock, explore your innermost thoughts. How would you confront these profound inquiries?

Moreover, what significance do the shimmering colors within the banshee's tears hold? Share your interpretation of this narrative and the revelations it unlocks within you.

I am grateful for:

1. _____

2. _____

3. _____

I acknowledge that mistakes and pain do not define me. I am the source of my healing and resilience.

Day 14: Spooktacular Self-Love

As the haunting days creep ever closer, it's the perfect time to immerse yourself in a night of spine-tingling excitement. Take a moment to choose a spooky or suspenseful movie you've been eagerly anticipating. Grab your favorite snacks, some popcorn, and a cozy blanket, and settle in for an evening of chilling entertainment.

Once the credits have rolled at the end, share the details of your night, describing how this act of self-love during this eerie season amplified the thrill of your experience.

What spooky movie did you select?

_____

- Describe the atmosphere and your feelings as you settled in for your movie night.
- How did your favorite snacks complement this spooky experience?
- How did this experience bring about a unique sense of self-love and delight?

I am grateful for:

1. _____

2. _____

3. _____

My heart beats with excitement, fueled by the powerful embrace of self-love.

Day 15: Soulful Whirls of the Magic Orb

Suppose you are house-sitting for your sorceress friend, who's off on a retreat with other mythical beings. As you wander through her pumpkin cottage, you explore fascinating shelves filled with potions, spell books, and mystical objects. Among them, a shiny crystal ball catches your attention. You are taken aback as you place it before you, for it extends an unexpected invitation. The radiant words within the orb read as follows:

"Gaze into the glass to reveal the soul who has etched the deepest mark upon your journey."

Whose face would you see in the depths of the crystal ball? What scenes would it project on its surface? Explore the significance of these glimpses and the profound messages they convey. What revelations arise as you immerse yourself in these memories?

I am grateful for:

1. _____

2. _____

3. _____

By embracing the lessons within my memories, I step into a future filled with clarity.

Day 16: Burial of Illusions

In an isolated cemetery, an array of weathered tombstones bear your name, though the birth and death dates are obscured. The atmosphere is heavy with an impending storm, and you stand before freshly dug graves, ready to bury certain aspects of your ego.

As you stand in this gloomy graveyard with the clouds gathering overhead, describe the inscriptions on the tombstones. Are there other mourners who have gathered to pay their respects? How does it feel to bid farewell to these facets of yourself?

Furthermore, what kind of eulogy would you give, and what realizations does it evoke as you recite it aloud?

I am grateful for:

1. _____

2. _____

3. _____

I release false illusions, making space for my true self to shine.

Day 17: Echoes of Childhood

Envision yourself waking up in an abandoned version of your childhood home. The rooms are filled with forgotten toys, mementos, and reminders of your past. What do you see around you, and what significance does this place hold for you? Furthermore, consider what this encounter reveals about the person you've become.

I am grateful for:

1. _____

2. _____

3. _____

I unlock treasures about my journey within each cherished memory.

Day 18: Mystical Wisdom

Step into the realm of self-reflection, where a collection of magical objects awaits your exploration. Imagine the following items arrayed on a table before you. Consider the one that resonates most with you—reflect on the reasons behind this connection and what it represents to you personally.

If this item had the ability to convey a message to you today, what would it say? (If none of the following items align with you, feel free to choose a different object for self-reflection.)

Cloak of Invisibility   Enchanted Mirror   Magical Ring   Witch's Broomstick

I am grateful for:

1. _____

2. _____

3. _____

I embrace my unique creative expression, allowing it to flow freely and authentically.

Day 19: A Haunting Reflection

If your reflection in the mirror suddenly grinned back at you with a sinister smile, what chilling yet fiercely empowering declarations would it confront you with? Furthermore, what response would you give your reflection?

I am grateful for:

1. _____

2. _____

3. _____

Fear is but an illusion, fading as I step into my authentic power.

Day 20: Boo

Imagine receiving a mysterious text message inviting you to "Spooky Brews & Tea House." The invitation—addressed to you personally by name, is signed by an enigmatic Boo, who provides a peculiar instruction:

"At the stroke of 3am, enter the portal that awakens beyond your closet door."

As the hands of the clock strike 3am, a soft radiance seeps through the crevices of your closet. With a mixture of trepidation and curiosity, you grasp the doorknob, open the door, and step forward. Before your eyes, instead of your closet, a café buzzes with translucent beings—and while mesmerized by this otherworldly manifestation, you, too, become a spirit, blending into the crowd.

A bit unsettled and out of your element, you approach the counter and order your favorite beverage. You discover that in this dimension, money is irrelevant; items manifest instantly upon request.

As you settle down to enjoy your drink, you gaze around the room, absorbing this incredible spectacle and eavesdropping on all kinds of ghostly chatter. Among them, certain spirits debate whether to move toward the light. Others share stories about those they've spooked and speculate about their next target. Some apparently lack all memory of their identity and the circumstances that befell them, leading them to this realm. And then there are those who yearn to communicate with their loved ones on the physical plane but are unable to reach them.

Enveloped by these captivating scenes, without warning, you are suddenly covered in goosebumps. A presence is seated across from you, intriguingly staring, and you have zero recollection of their arrival. After a few seconds, the ghost admits to sending the invitation by text, and proceeds with an offer:

"I will answer three questions about a specific soul that occupies your thoughts. In return, I ask you to deliver a message to those I love in your realm of existence."

Would you strike a deal with a ghost? And if so, what three questions would you pose about the person in your mind? Moreover, do you have any clues regarding the identity of this phantom? You are welcome to choose the figure that best personifies Boo in your mind.

I am grateful for:

1. _____

2. _____

3. _____

HI

YOU ARE INVITED TO
SPOOKY BREWS & TEA HOUSE.

@ 3AM

ENTER THE PORTAL THAT
AWAKENS BEYOND YOUR
CLOSET DOOR.

BOO.

My life is full of whimsical love stories, each one more magical than the last.

Day 21: Pumpkin Zen

Today, you are invited to embrace a moment of mindfulness by engaging creatively with a pumpkin. This activity will root you in the present moment, enabling creative expression and fostering self-connection. Go seek out a lovely pumpkin and let your imagination run wild.

As you immerse yourself in this creative pursuit, let your artistry and innovation flow without judgment or expectation. This mindfulness exercise is intended to help you revel in the here and now, attuning yourself to tactile sensations, vibrant colors, earthly scents, and soothing sounds.

You are welcome to design your pumpkin in any way you desire. Here are a few suggestions to spark your creativity:

Paint it: Use your pumpkin as a canvas, painting it with a vibrant palette of colors. Convey your feelings and imagination with every stroke.

Decorate it: Gather an array of decorative items such as ribbons, glitter, stickers, or tiny trinkets. Adorn your pumpkin with these materials using glue or string, activating your sensory perception as you carefully arrange your items.

Carve it: If you appreciate a more tactile experience, utilize carving tools to sculpt a design or a face into your pumpkin. Notice the sounds, scents, and textures as you carve through the pumpkin's flesh.

Write on it: Express your thoughts or gratitude by writing directly on the pumpkin's surface with markers or pens. Let the power of your words resound, grounding yourself in the present moment.

Nature-Inspired: If you prefer a more natural approach, venture outdoors to gather leaves, twigs, flowers, and other natural elements. Arrange these treasures on your pumpkin, creating a piece of art that nurtures a connection with the earth.

I am grateful for:

1. _____

2. _____

3. _____

I release judgment and embrace the flow of my creativity, making space for inspiration and innovation.

Day 22: Shifting Realms

While wandering through the hallways of an eerie hospital where haunting creatures are treated, no one seems to notice your presence, as if you yourself were a ghost within this realm. As you continue your exploration, your intuition leads you to the ICU, where you find yourself outside the rooms of three patients, each in critical condition.

The first room is occupied by a battered werewolf covered in bandages; he was attacked and beaten by a pack of ruthless humans. In the next room lies a zombie surrounded by loved ones; she bit the wrong human and contracted a deadly disease. Lastly, you find yourself before the headless horseman who experienced a terrible fall from his horse. Now in a coma, his headless wife weeps quietly beside his bed.

Standing shocked outside the three rooms, you hear a voice speak in your mind. In a calm, unconcerned tone, it asks you the following questions:

"Do you believe the fate of every individual's death is predetermined?"

"Can death be viewed as a graduation for the soul?"

"What are your reflections on what happens after death? Does the learning process end, or does it continue in some form?"

Take a moment to contemplate the questions posed by the mysterious voice and explore your views regarding these profound perspectives. Moreover, what kind of voice do you imagine speaking to you as you ponder the depths of death within your existence?

I am grateful for:

1. _____

2. _____

3. _____

I trust in the wisdom and growth of my soul's journey, including the transitions of life and death.

Day 23: Word Quest

PALPITATION

Take a moment to contemplate the given word. What thoughts, emotions, images, or desires does it evoke within you?

I am grateful for:

1. _____

2. _____

3. _____

The thrill of excitement pulses through me, attracting moments that cast a glow on my soul.

Day 24: Twyla's Twilight Treats

As you enjoy a walk in the twilight hours, an unexpected sweet scent wafts through the air, kindling your curiosity. You turn to find a mysterious figure by a quaint, old-fashioned stand—a witch, patiently waiting with hypnotic allure. Her eyes glimmer with unearthly light, and her unsettling smile suggests a hidden secret.

Intrigued, you approach to investigate this peculiar character and her wares. In a tone that sends shivers down your spine, she introduces herself as Twyla and extends a caramel apple.

"Would you like an apple?" she asks. "Its delicious, sweet taste can grant the youth you desire and slow the aging process."

You take the apple, finding yourself captivated by its tempting, appetizing features, when she adds a chilling caveat:

"However, consuming the apple reduces your lifespan by six years."

The decision is yours to make. Would you consume a poisoned apple, trading years for youth? Why or why not?

Contemplate the concept of impermanence. Reflect on the aspects of aging that evoke gratitude, and consider the gifts that growing older has bestowed upon you. How might the witch's proposal influence your current choices and perspective on the significance of self-appreciation through your aging journey?

I am grateful for:

1. _____

2. _____

3. _____

I embrace the beauty that comes with the passage of time.

Day 25: A Spooky Farmers Market

Imagine a dimly lit farmers market nestled within the outskirts of a small, eerie town. The stalls are adorned with real hanging bats, twisted pumpkins, and floating candles while ghostly music plays in the distance, orchestrated by invisible hands.

As you walk through this unusual scene, a cast of spooky vendors offer you a range of mysterious treats.

A ghost offers you "Bubble Gum Boo," claiming each strip turns you invisible as long as you chew.

A werewolf presents "Moonlight Pops," assuring that these little, radiant orbs on sticks will make you glow like the moon.

A Mummy tempts you with "Gummy Eyes," stating that these sweets will help you maintain an optimistic view through any situation.

A little black cat, stationed at a booth with a small inkpad by its side, offers you a stamp of its paw. This inky imprint will allow you to possess night vision and a purring ability lasting up to three full moons. This purring power facilitates meditation and generates healing vibrations.

Lastly, a skeleton draped in a doctor's coat with a stethoscope around his neck asks whether you desire to know your "expiration date."

Now that you've witnessed these unusual and wondrous proposals, which of these extraordinary treats would you choose, and what adventures would you embark on with your newfound abilities or knowledge? Reflect on your choices and the reasons behind them.

I am grateful for:

1. _____

2. _____

3. _____

Every day, I make unique and exciting choices.

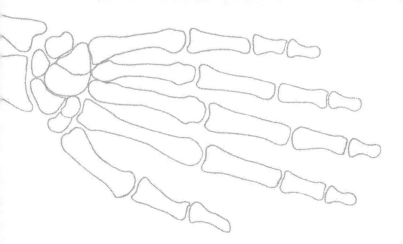

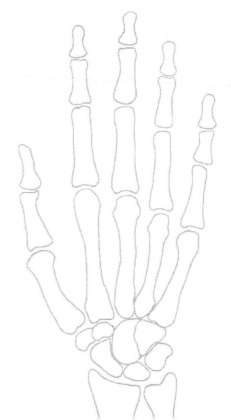

Day 26: The Enigma of I

Suppose you receive a mysterious invitation to a masquerade ball, hosted in a secluded mansion. As you put on your mask and attend the event, you are astonished to find that every other guest, some of whom you recognize, wears a mask of your face. What does this strange gathering unveil about your innermost self and the facades you display?

I am grateful for:

1. _____

2. _____

3. _____

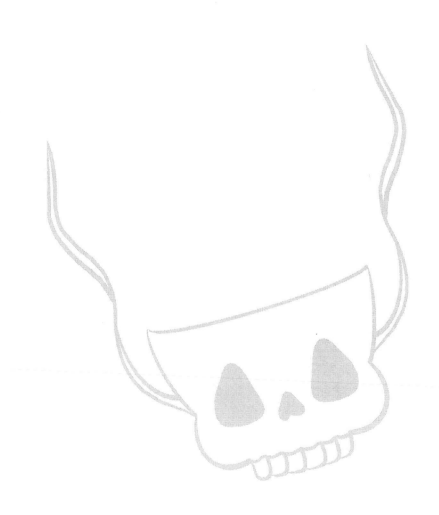

My self-awareness deepens with every masquerade.

Day 27: Finding Beauty in Darkness

In a cryptic world where haunting creatures roam the streets, one peculiar being captures your attention. She is an artist painting a magnificent portrait filled with color, details, and depth. Puzzled by the contrast between the unsettling surroundings and the delicate beauty she creates, you approach and inquire about her painting.

She introduces herself as Tiger and explains that her art is inspired by and born from challenging times, and is intended to awaken other souls to the healing power of creativity.

Pause for a moment to consider this perspective. Can you find a connection between hardship and creative inspiration? How has creativity manifested itself through moments of darkness, illuminating your path toward acceptance and deep insight?

How does Tiger's story influence your thoughts? Do you believe there's a greater picture to be found amidst the fragments of your life? Take a moment to pen down your reflections inspired by this narrative.

I am grateful for:

1. _____

2. _____

3. _____

I acknowledge the beauty of my journey, finding strength in both joyous and challenging moments.

Day 28: Orio's Search

When you arrive home, you find an abandoned toy on your doorstep: a black-and-white bear lying on the ground with unusual, glassy buttons for eyes. After a moment of consideration, you leave the stuffed animal outside, thinking you can deal with it later.

You enter the kitchen to make a cup of coffee, and when you turn around, you are startled to find the bear is now seated at the eating table. In a composed manner, it shares the following:

"Greetings, my name is Orio. You've been selected to participate in a human survey—I would like to ask you a few questions."

Astonished yet intrigued by this uncanny encounter, you grab your coffee and join Orio at the table. Despite offering him a cup, he politely declines and proceeds with the following questions (recording your responses through his illuminating eyes):

"Have you encountered unconditional love in this existence? If so, in what ways have you experienced it, and what valuable insights have you gained from unconditional love?"

"Alternatively, what insights and lessons have you gained from the realm of conditional love? What does it feel like, and in what ways has it influenced your behavior?"

"Lastly, are there specific areas in which you'd like to further expand unconditional self-love, and what outcomes do you envision resulting from this pursuit?"

Take a moment to sip your coffee while you ponder these profound questions posed by the unearthly bear, and jot down your reflections.

I am grateful for:

1. _____

2. _____

3. _____

I open myself to the flow of unconditional love, embracing the freedom to give and receive it.

Day 29: The Enchanting Graveyard

Imagine a secret cemetery hidden in a secluded corner of town. Within this extraordinary place, enchantment and celebration of life fill the air, casting aside sorrow and gloom. Each gravestone is adorned with colorful flowers, whimsical ornaments, and twinkling lights, telling a unique story. As you explore this mystical site, you notice one grave in particular. The inscription on the tombstone captures your attention, offering a profound and thought-provoking message.

What does the inscription say? As you ponder the significance of the words, contemplate life's most profound and meaningful aspects. What revelations does this narrative awaken within you? Moreover, what words would you desire to be etched on your own headstone?

I am grateful for:

1. _____

2. _____

3. _____

I spread laughter like fairy dust, transforming each moment into a celebration.

When you're
Done with old
Shoes,
Youl'll get
New ones.
E. A. Z.

Day 30: The Midnight Cauldron

As the clock strikes midnight, an old Western tavern materializes out of thin air. Shocked and confused by the sudden transition, you realize you are seated at a bar in pajamas. A sign by a row of shelved potions features the name "The Midnight Cauldron." As you look around, you witness several haunting activities:

A group of gooey, green beings with dark glasses gaze at you momentarily before continuing their poker game, the cards sticky with their residue.

Near the entrance, a familiar skeleton expertly plays the piano, his bony fingers clacking on the keys, filling the air with jaunty, spooky tunes.

In the very darkest corner of the tavern, a mist-covered wendigo looms ominously, with hollowed eyes fixated on something unseen.

A pumpkin scarecrow and his lady companion sit at a candlelit table, sipping Cauldron Coolers and savoring a sweet potato pie.

Over at the bar, the Grim Reaper enjoys a Morgue-a-Rita as he reviews his to-do list for the night with an unsettling smile.

While you gape in a moment of eerie astonishment, the bartender approaches. His skin is pale, and his smile is sharply fanged. He places a glass of blood-red wine before you, and in a chilling voice, he shares the following:

"A single sip of the wine will unveil your future."

Would you take a sip of the foretelling wine? Why or why not? Contemplate your decision and share the reasoning behind your choice.

I am grateful for:

1. _____

2. _____

3. _____

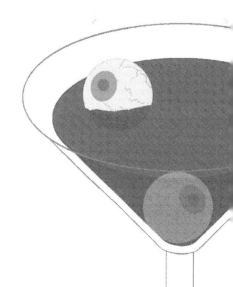

I trust in the journey ahead, confident that my path leads toward a future filled with abundance.

Day 31: Trick or Treat?

While enjoying an all-time favorite scary film, your doorbell suddenly rings. You look through the peephole to see who visits, but no one stands at the door. A bit perturbed by the situation, you cautiously open the door and peek around for a clearer view. Shockingly, a live scarecrow stands before you. "Trick or treat!" it exclaims. Both intrigued and spooked by the scarecrow's appearance, you reach for the candy bowl and offer it a treat. But instead of taking the candy, the scarecrow repeats, "Trick or treat?" it becomes evident it awaits a response.

Before proceeding, contemplate your decision. Make your pick and fill in your answer below. Once you've decided, continue reading ahead for the outcome of your choice.

_____

If you chose "Treat":

The scarecrow hands you a small bag of candy corn. When eaten, these candies immediately alleviate any anxiety. You taste one, and a sense of calmness envelops you, protecting you from fear and negativity. How might you strategically use these treats to navigate difficult days and circumstances? Furthermore, consider what strategies you might employ during distressing moments. Create a list of helpful techniques, keeping them close to you. If and when anxiety emerges, refer to your list and engage in one of these techniques as though you were indulging in a sweet little kernel. This practice can serve as a comforting resource, offering support and guidance whenever you need it most.

If you chose "Trick":

The scarecrow hands you a bag of shimmering, white gummy worms. As you consume one of the gummies, you feel a strange sensation on your teeth. A label suddenly appears on the bag, revealing that these sweets cause acute sensitivity to blame and self-pity. Thus, your teeth will rot when you blame others and fall prey to cycles of self-victimization. Alternatively, embracing an empowering stance will cleanse your teeth, keeping your smile bright. The effects of these gummy worms will last until the scarecrow's next visit during the spooky season. How might these gummies influence your perception of resilience while empowering your smile?

Whichever choice you make, envision how it might shape your experiences and reactions. How might you adapt to the effects of these peculiar treats?

I am grateful for:

1. _____

2. _____

3. _____

In the stillness of my mind, I find a wellspring of resilience that empowers me to navigate challenges with a calm and steady heart.

Final Echoes of the Haunting Season

As we draw the curtains on this spooky chapter of the year, take a moment to reflect on any meaningful revelations that transpired during this haunting season while appreciating any transformation you experienced within. In life's unpredictable twists and turns, may you persist in celebrating your potential, finding light even in the darkest moments. Let the lessons gained here fill your heart with delight, new insight, and self-empowerment. And as you continue unraveling the mysteries of your enigmatic soul, look forward to embracing the spirit and warmth of the harvest season.

Made in the USA
Columbia, SC
17 July 2024

4b196036-13db-4553-b6fb-d9b7700e2158R01